Exploring Midsomer

The Towns and Villages at the Murderous Heart of England

Chris Behan

Dedicated to my grandchildren, Ella and Joshua

Front Cover: Aldbury village green, featured in 'Written in Blood'.
Back Cover: Brill Windmill at Sunset.

First published 2012

The History Press
The Mill, Brimscombe Port
Stroud, Gloucestershire, GL5 2QG
www.thehistorypress.co.uk

British Library Cataloguing in Publication Data.
A catalogue record for this book is available from the British Library.

ISBN 978 0 7524 6223 3

Typesetting and origination by The History Press
Printed in Spain

Opposite Page: St Mary the Virgin, Hambleden Church, featured in 'Blood will out'.

CONTENTS

Foreword   5

Introduction   6

Acknowledgements   7

Buckinghamshire   9

Oxfordshire   11

The Chiltern Hills   13

The Thames Valley   15

Aylesbury Vale   17

White Ducks and Witchert Walls   19
Brill, Chearsley, Cuddington, Dinton, Haddenham,
Long Crendon, Waddesdon

The Ridgeway National Trail   33
The Ridgeway, Bledlow, Cadsden, Watlington, Lewknor

Along the Oxfordshire Motorway   39
Great and Little Haseley, Thame, Oxford

Red Kites and the Vicar of Dibley   45
Red Kites, Wormsley Park, Stonor Manor, Turville, Nettlebed

Pooh Sticks, Clumps and an Abbey   51
Brightwell Baldwin, Britwell Salome, Dorchester-on-Thames,
Ewelme, Warborough, Wallingford

Port, Pimms and Wine   59
Henley-on-Thames, Marlow, Hambleden, Aston and Remenham, Hurley

A Royal Castle and a Racecourse   67
Bray, Windsor and Eton, Littlewick Green

Beech Woods and Commons   73
Burnham Beeches, Beaconsfield

The River Chess Valley   77
The River Chess, Chesham, Chenies and Latimer, Flauden, Sarratt

The River Misbourne and Metroland   83
Amersham, Little and Great Missenden

Chiltern Hundreds and Thousands   87
Chiltern Hundreds, Aldbury, The Lee

Preservation Railway Lines   91
Chinnor and Princes Risborough Railway
and Buckinghamshire Railway Centre

Maps   94

FOREWORD

I am delighted that my friend Chris has invited me to write a foreword to this superb collection of photographs that get right to the heart of the lethal but fortunately fictional land of 'Midsomer'. I have known Chris for over twenty years and have seen his photography develop over that time to a truly professional level, combining superb artistry and an ability to 'see' and compose his photographs that I envy greatly. He has taught me much of what I know in photography to a level that many of my books and articles carry my own photographs.

As he writes in his Introduction he has lived in the heart of 'Midsomer' for decades, although observing fewer murders than Inspector Barnaby. I too have lived in 'Midsomer' for well over thirty years and my village of Haddenham has featured many times.

Over the years Chris and I have played location spotting and when preparing the photographs for this book he gave me a taxing time trying to identify where he had taken some of the views. Many of his photographs in this beautiful book are recognisable and are of well-known locations such as Waddesdon Manor or Brill's famous windmill; others less so. However, some of his broader landscape photographs such as the expansive and vast views interspersed within the text are simply outstanding and completely breathtaking. He has captured some wonderful cloud formations while some detailed shots are far more intimate, for example the head of one of the famous Aylesbury ducks that were once common in the Vale or individual wild flowers.

I think the 'Midsomer' team is exceptionally fortunate in being able to set its stories in such a beautiful part of the world.

As a professional walker I have walked most of the footpaths in the 'Midsomer' area and never tire of the countryside, the fine market towns and the villages. This book is a superb pictorial tribute both to 'Midsomer', the Chilterns, Aylesbury Vale and the Thames Valley.

Martin Andrew,
Former Manager, Design and Conservation at Wycombe District Council
Author of the Collins' *Rambler's Guide Chilterns and Ridgeway* and the AA's
50 Walks in Hertfordshire
Haddenham, November 2011

INTRODUCTION

Midsomer Murders is one of those long-running and very successful television series. Like *Last of the Summer Wine*, it is English through and through. It is thatched cottages, old parish churches, cricket on the green, village institutions, summer church fêtes, duck ponds and the local inn.

It is a classic English 'who dunnit', in the fingerprints of Agatha Christie, who lived and is buried in Wallingford, the spiritual county town of 'Midsomer'. However, it has more murders and is much more bloody than any Agatha Christie novel.

The gentility of the county of 'Midsomer' compares starkly with the savagery of the crimes committed behind the lace curtains of its villages.

The pleasures of watching *Midsomer Murders* are two-fold: to see the beautiful villages and countryside in which the series is filmed and the challenge of trying to solve the crime before 'Inspector Barnaby' does. Yes, we know 'Inspector Barnaby' will solve, almost single-handedly, the murders. He only solves murders! Is there no other crime committed in 'Midsomer'?

Midsomer Murders is set in the English counties of Buckinghamshire and Oxfordshire with an occasional visit over the borders to Berkshire, Hertfordshire and the odd place further afield. In geographical terms, it is the Chilterns, the Aylesbury Vale and the Thames Valley, areas of outstanding natural beauty in which I have had the pleasure of living for nearly forty years.

I have concentrated on the more interesting villages and smaller market towns which illustrate the English countryside at its best. As always, there is an exception. I have included the City of Oxford, despite the fact that nearly everything that could be written about the city has been written. However, there is a much-overlooked attraction in the city and it has not been overlooked by *Midsomer Murders*.

The book has been divided into chapters, each for a group of locations that are close together and have a common external link. I hope this will make for a more interesting read, but more importantly, the basis for planning visits to the counties of Buckinghamshire and Oxfordshire.

It goes without exception that I am an enthusiastic fan of the counties of Buckinghamshire and Oxfordshire and the fictional 'Midsomer'. I hope this book, in my words and photographs taken over many years, conveys this enthusiasm. Enjoy it, then take a day out and appreciate the real 'Midsomer', but be ever watchful. Remember, it may be beautiful but 'Midsomer' is the murder capital of England!

ACKNOWLEDGEMENTS

Thanks to, in no particular order:

Liz, my sister, who let her little brother in short trousers use her 35mm camera and photograph trains in colour using the original Kodachrome slide film. For those of you who can remember, it was a very slow film (ASA 10) and I soon discovered that the train had to be stationary or otherwise it was a blur. Things got better with the introduction of Kodachrome II in 1961.

My friends in the Rotary Club of Haddenham and District who have always encouraged me, not that it was needed, to create a photographic record of the club's history over the past twenty-five years. If ever a Rotary Club deserved to be 'The Rotary Club of Midsomer', this is the one. Its members live in eight 'Midsomer' villages, and many of their homes, including mine, have been seen in the series; one member even arrived home to find a 'body' on his doorstep. He has the 'murder weapon' to prove it, presented to him by the *Midsomer Murders* production team.

Martin Andrew, who knows more than I will ever know, especially about Buckinghamshire and Oxfordshire, a subject on which he has written many books. Martin pointed me in the right direction when I was lost, to discover buildings and sites in 'Midsomer'.

Despite living in a 'first to have the latest gadget' home, there are occasions when technical support is required. Appreciation and tremendous thanks go to my two great sons, Nik and Kevin. Nik, who has a degree in Design and Photography, which helps, answers all the photography and Photoshop calls for help, whilst Kevin, the whiz-kid with computer hardware and software, is always on hand to keep the production flowing.

Rarely do I read acknowledgements to the producers of all the nuts and bolts that enable artists, writers and photographers to create. In my case, a special thank you goes to Apple, Adobe and Canon who have produced great computers, software and photographic equipment. Their products have liberated the latent creative talent of ordinary people and enabled them to produce great works.

An unusual vote of thanks must go to Hugh Jones, author of *The Chiltern Railways Story* published by The History Press. He included a photograph of mine in his book, fortunately for me without acknowledgement, which was how I was introduced to The History Press. This particular story now becomes unreal. Stuart Biles, the managing director of The History Press, invited me to the company's offices. Armed with the titles of twelve books I would like to see published, I met publisher Amy Rigg. Ten titles quickly ended in the bin but two survived and this book is one of the two. A very special thanks must, therefore, go to Stuart, Amy, Emily, Jemma and the staff of The History Press for giving me this great opportunity. A million thanks.

Finally the biggest thanks goes to Margaret, my wife, who suffered me vanishing into the study to tap away on my Apple Mac for hours, days, weeks and months on end.

To my family, all the above people and everyone who has helped me, encouraged me and inspired me, a very big thank you!

Chris Behan

(No, Roger, I am not applying to *Mastermind* with the specialised subject being 'Midsomer'!)

Ridgeway sheep.

BUCKINGHAMSHIRE

Vestigia nulla retrorsum – 'No retreat'

Buckinghamshire was frontier territory 1,000 or so years ago, the eastern edge of the Saxon kingdom of Wessex. The county's boundaries were set by the tenth-century warlords and tax collectors, whose task was to find the men and money to fight off the invading Danes.

Buckinghamshire's greatest person, John Hampden, was a key figure in the English Civil War and his impact on English democratic history cannot be overstated. He was not a revolutionary but a moderate patriotic character who wished that the rights and privileges of each man, as well as Parliament, should be respected. It is Hampden whose statue was selected by the Victorians to take its place at the entrance to the Central Lobby in the Palace of Westminster as a symbol of the noblest type of the parliamentary opposition, sword at his side, ready to defend Parliament's rights and privileges by any means necessary. His statue also stands in Aylesbury's Market Square and he is depicted in the Aylesbury Vale District Council logo.

Nowadays, Buckinghamshire, a contrasting landscape of tranquil countryside and lively towns with the meandering River Thames and the rolling Chiltern Hills, is home for celebrities working in London.

Buckinghamshire is famous for furniture and lace. The Windsor chair is made from the beech tree that grows locally in the Chiltern Hills and is named after Windsor Castle, which, by the way, is not in the county but on the other side of the River Thames in Berkshire. Bucks Point Lace is straight lace, traditionally made with fine thread.

The Rothschild family has had more impact on the landscape of Buckinghamshire than any other landowner. They purchased or built five properties in the county during the nineteenth century, including Waddesdon Manor, built by Baron Ferdinand de Rothschild to display his outstanding collection of art treasures and to entertain the fashionable world.

Right: Mature trees in Waddesdon Manor.

Britwell Hill, locally known as 'Chitty Chitty Bang Bang Hill', Britwell Salome.

OXFORDSHIRE

Fortis est veritas – 'Truth is strength'

Founded in the West Saxon kingdom of Mercia in 1007, Oxfordshire was a dangerous, violent place 1,000 years ago, as Danes and Anglo-Saxons struggled for supremacy over much of England.

Oxfordshire has come a long way since then. The most rural county in South East England, it presents a quintessentially English picture of the countryside, scattered with market towns, villages, churches, historic routes and a city.

Oxfordshire has been birthplace and home to countless significant individuals. King Alfred the Great, Edward the Confessor, Richard I, King John and Hadrian IV, England's first and only Pope.

A land of learning, invention and production, Oxfordshire is known for Cotswold wool, Witney blankets, Woodstock gloves, Stonesfield slate, Banbury Cakes, BMW Minis and Renault and Williams Formula 1 racing cars.

Home to university scholarship since the twelfth century and book printing since the fifteenth century, Oxford has more published writers per square mile than anywhere else in the world, and almost as many distinguished scientists. The English language, in the form of the Oxford English Dictionary, is its most internationally famous export.

The Oxford Plain, home to well over ten 'Midsomer' towns and villages and one city.

The ancient Whiteleaf Cross in the Chiltern Hills overlooking the Ridgeway and Cadsden.

THE CHILTERN HILLS

The Chilterns, as the Chiltern Hills are known locally, is a beautiful, unspoilt corner of England, mainly in parts of Oxfordshire and Buckinghamshire. Despite its closeness to London, the Chilterns have a very rural character devoid of modern suburban growth.

Its gently rolling hills are swathed in ancient beech woodlands, which provide a haven for wildlife. They are home to a number of rare orchids, many species of fungi, the rare dormouse and the red kite. *Midsomer Murders* has taken advantage of the orchids and the fungi in the storyline of two episodes, 'Orchis Fatalis' and 'Destroying Angel'. A visit in May to see the stunning displays of bluebells is a must.

The chalk downlands are the source of eight chalk streams, Hughenden Stream, Hambleden Brook and the Rivers Ver, Gade, Bulbourne, Chess, Misbourne and Wye. These streams, with a steady flow of clean, mineral-rich spring water at a constant 10°C, support some of our most threatened species, the water vole and the white-clawed crayfish, as well as being ideal for watercress production.

In the valleys of the chalk streams, attractive villages with traditional brick and flint cottages and welcoming pubs and inns nestle around medieval churches. Ancient tracks and byways, the oldest being the Ridgeway, cross the area, giving a sense of the history that has unfolded in the Chilterns.

During the nineteenth century the woods were full of bodgers, not the modern clumsy DIY enthusiast, but skilled chair leg turners who made components for Windsor chairs, manufactured locally around High Wycombe.

Spring in the Chiltern woodlands. A rare white English bluebell.

Spring in the Chiltern woodlands. A false oxslip.

Thames Valley with Dorchester-on-Thames in the distance.

THE THAMES VALLEY

The source of the River Thames is in the Cotswolds, near Kemble, Gloucestershire. Its journey to the North Sea passes through peaceful water meadows, unspoilt rural villages, historic towns and cities, and finally through London. However, the only area surrounding the river that is referred to as 'The Thames Valley' is from Oxfordshire in the west to the approaches of London in the east, which includes, as well as Oxfordshire, parts of Buckinghamshire and Berkshire.

It is one of Britain's most beautiful regions with attractions ranging from sun-dappled woodlands to wild flower-covered chalk downs, from thatched cottages to ancient buildings and from bustling market towns to quaint villages. And let us not forget the many village pubs and inns, which serve good ales, good wines and good food.

Whilst Oxford is the most well-known city, Henley-on-Thames, Marlow, Maidenhead and Reading are all important places in the Thames Valley.

Henley-on-Thames is, perhaps, the best known of these four towns because of its world-renowned annual Royal Rowing Regatta.

River Thames, near Hambleden Lock.

Aerial view of Aylesbury Vale. Haddenham Village, centre left.

AYLESBURY VALE

The Aylesbury Vale stretches across open plains of rural grassland with a mixture of arable, livestock and dairy farms. Its boundary is marked by Milton Keynes to the north, the Chiltern Hills to the east and south, Thame (Oxfordshire) to the south and Bicester (Oxfordshire) and Brackley (Northamptonshire) to the west. Scattered with bustling market towns and rural villages, the Vale still has more than 350 square miles of unspoilt countryside. The bed of the Vale is largely made up of clays, formed at the end of the ice age, the most significant of these clays being Witchert, a white clay. The white clay is found only around the village of Haddenham and neighbouring villages, where, for centuries, it has been used as a building material.

The Vale is named after the historic town of Aylesbury, the county town of Buckinghamshire. Appropriately Aylesbury, famous for its breed of white duck with its distinctive flesh-pink beak, is twinned with the French town Bourg-en-Bresse, famous for its breed of chicken, the Poulet de Bresse, with its distinctive red crown, white feathers and blue feet.

The French connection does not end there. The Rothschilds settled in the Vale around Waddesdon where Baron Ferdinand de Rothschild, between 1874 and 1889, built Waddesdon Manor in the Neo-Renaissance style of a French château.

Earlier, between 1810 and 1814, the Jacobean mansion of Hartwell, near Aylesbury, was the residence of the French King Louis XVIII during the last part of his twenty-three years in exile following the French Revolution. Louis's wife, Marie Josephine of Savoy, died at Hartwell in 1810 and is buried in the churchyard. She is the only French Queen to be buried on English soil.

The Vale's ancient woodland trails and rolling hills are perfect for walking and horse riding, with more than 1,000 miles of footpaths and bridle paths.

Aylesbury Vale looking towards Waddesdon Manor on the distant hill.

Pekin, not Aylesbury, ducks on Church End Green, Haddenham.

White Ducks and Witchert Walls

Aylesbury Ducks

Sadly the Aylesbury duck, all white with a flesh pink-coloured beak, is a threatened species and the last surviving flock of pure Aylesbury ducks in the country can only be found at a farm near Chesham. The white ducks, which can be seen on village ponds, are white Pekin ducks, distinguishable from the Aylesbury duck by their yellow beaks.

Witchert Walls

Four of the villages, Chearsley, Cuddington, Haddenham and Long Crendon, lie on a layer of unusual white clay. This clay is used as a local building material and is known as Witchert. A Witchert wall is constructed on a foundation of stones, the grumpling. The wall is then built up with layers of the white clay, straw and rubble. Finally, the top of the wall is covered with thatch or tiles to protect it and the Aylesbury ducks from the rain.

A real Aylesbury duck with flesh-pink beak.

A Witchert wall.

Brill Common and its windmill featured in 'A Tale of Two Hamlets'. The mill was 'Sarah Proudie's' home.

BRILL

The original invading Celtic settlers called the site of the village 'Bre', Celt for 'hill'. However, by the time the Anglo-Saxons had pushed the Celts to the far corners of the British Isles in the sixth and seventh centuries, the origin of the name 'Bre' had been forgotten. So, the Anglo-Saxons renamed the settlement, 'Bre Hyll'. Two hills are better than one! Nowadays an avenue in Brill carries this Anglo-Saxon name, Brae Hill.

Brill stands 400ft above the Aylesbury Vale and the Thames Valley at a height of just over 600ft above sea level. A perfect site for prehistoric, Celtic, Roman (it is only 3 miles from the Roman road, Akeman Street), Anglo-Saxon and modern commuter settlements.

Prior to the construction of Windsor Castle, the Kings of England went to Brill Castle for relaxation and recreation, no doubt hunting in nearby Bernwode Forest.

Nine Kings came to Brill, from William I to Richard I. However, by the thirteenth century Brill Castle had lost its attraction for the Royals. They preferred a residence closer to London and Brill Castle was eventually abandoned in 1327; Windsor's gain and Brill's loss.

The village could not be classified as one of the most beautiful in England, but it has amazing views. On a clear day seven English counties can be seen, especially from the pitted common, which gives us a clue as to its lack of charm. The common is clay, the raw material for brick making, which brought Brill its wealth. The pitted common? The result of clay extraction.

Sadly, the brick makers were unable to take advantage of the Industrial Revolution. The common went back to nature but the legacy of Brill bricks can be seen in the decorative brick walls and tiled roofs that cover the old daub and wattle structures and thatched roofs of the old village cottages. Nearby Waddesdon Manor was built using the village bricks.

Brill is best known for its seventeenth-century post windmill (I used to be a guide on Sunday afternoons) located on the common, which has starred in film, television series and advertisements.

Midsomer Murders is not the only crime to be associated with Brill. Leatherslade Farm, in Brill parish, was the base for the Great Train Robbery in 1963. Brill Magistrates Court (now domestic residences) was their first port of call after being arrested.

Brill All Saints Church and The Green, the setting for the 'Skimmington Ride', a traditional custom expressing a public demonstration of moral disapproval featured in 'Four Funerals and a Wedding'.

CHEARSLEY

'A small village in Buckinghamshire'

Chearsley is a small, attractive village which you can almost miss as it is established on the east side of the Crendon to Aylesbury road. The site slopes steeply down to the willow tree-lined River Thame but stopping short of the river as the meadows regularly flood after heavy rain.

One of the delights of Chearsley is that all the old residences in the meandering lanes have delightful and descriptive names such as 'Cobwebs', 'Bee Cottage', 'The Bobbins' in Turnip Close and 'High Bank' in Dark Lane.

With just over 200 period residences, a church, a post office general store and the Bell public house, the village makes an ideal location for filming and, no doubt, a question in future pub quizzes. Which village was the location for 'Inspector Tom Barnaby's' last *Midsomer Murders* investigation?

CUDDINGTON

'…is situated in a narrow alley north of the road from Aylesbury…'
George Lipscomb, 1847

Today, Cuddington is still 'situated in a narrow alley', probably better known as Upper Church Street. This does not do justice to a beautifully kept village with thatched white Witchert wall cottages, two greens, a church, the village shop and the Crown Inn, so much admired by the *Midsomer Murders'* production team.

The village hall, Bernard Hall, is widely used. I have been to quiz nights, amateur dramatics and even a wedding reception in the hall. In fact, probably more times than 'Inspector Barnaby'.

Cuddington prides itself in regularly being 'Best Kept Village in Buckinghamshire' and winning 'Britain in Bloom' awards.

The Bell Inn, Cheasley, 'The Woodman' in 'Country Matters'.

Best kept village, Cuddington.

Beautiful thatched cottage, Cuddington.

Bernard Hall, Cuddington. A local entertainment venue, it was also a 'Midsomer' venue for a Spanish Evening in 'Bad Tidings'.

Dinton.

DINTON

'Difficult to characterise'

Dinton is difficult to characterise. The exact location of the centre of the parish of Dinton can be somewhat confusing to the stranger as it comprises five hamlets: Dinton, Westlington, Upton, Ford and Gibraltar. This is not uncommon. Villages made up of several hamlets can be found elsewhere in this area. Originally the hamlets and Dinton Church were separated from each other by fields. The church is built on high ground with superb views across meadows looking towards the Chiltern Hills in the distance. The open area, with its postage stamp green around the church, contrasts with the more densely built-up area close to Westlington Green.

In the eleventh century the hamlets were in the ownership of the Norman Bishop of Bayeux, which resulted in the twentieth-century BBC *Mastermind* question 'Which quarry provided the stone to build Dinton Church?' Not surprisingly the answer is Caen quarry in Normandy, as the Normans built the vast majority of their castles and churches in Europe using stone from this quarry. Was it the quality of the sandstone chosen by the stonemasons or was it political and trade protectionism? The latter, I suggest. The Normans, obviously, handed down this trait to the Franks, as it is still evident in twenty-first-century French politics.

The French connection still remains today. The website of a château in the Dordogne, Château Gauthié, refers to the Westlington restaurant, 'La Chouette', as 'Buckinghamshire's best kept secret!' 'La Chouette', the little owl, is actually a Belgium restaurant. The food is very good, more French than Belgian, and the owner and chef can be entertaining. I would advise booking in advance. You can see the little owl inn sign in the *Midsomer Murders* episode 'Who killed Cock Robin?', when a body is pulled out of the village well on Westlington Green. Sadly the village well is purely fictional.

Next to the church is Dinton Hall, a much-renovated sixteenth-century house, whilst on the Aylesbury Road, a few yards from the church, is the ruin of a mock castle, Dinton Castle, constructed in 1769. As it is also known as Dinton Folly, I suggest it is only worth a glance as you drive by!

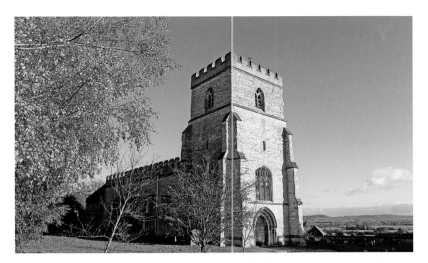

Dinton Church used for the wedding in 'Who Killed Cock Robin?'.

Westlington Green.

Old and new Haddenham Church End Green.

HADDENHAM

'Silly Haddenham who thatched the ponds to keep the ducks dry'

Haddenham is probably the largest village in Buckinghamshire. It is famous for its ponds. There are still four ponds in the village and the village claims to be the original breeding ground for the Aylesbury duck, the all–white ones with flesh-coloured beaks. Unfortunately, the ducks in Haddenham, which can be seen on the pond in front of the parish church, are yellow-beaked white Pekin ducks rather than the Aylesbury variety.

Haddenham is a Witchert village with its Witchert walls covered by thatch or tiles to protect them and the ducks from the rain. Hence, the old saying, 'Silly Haddenham who thatched the ponds to keep the ducks dry'. Fine examples of these walls can be seen all around the village and the Methodist Chapel is considered to be the largest Witchert-built building in the world.

With so much building heritage, it is not surprising that there are over 100 listed buildings in the village.

At the back of the church pond is the entrance to Church End Farm, which is nearly as old as the church. It has a fine tithe barn that is regularly used for local events.

Tiggywinkles, the world's busiest wildlife hospital, caring for over 10,000 sick and injured hedgehogs, badgers, wild birds, foxes, and even reptiles and amphibians every year, is located in the village. Visitors are welcome.

Haddenham has the distinction of being one of the few locations in *Midsomer Murders* which is referred to by its real name. The murderer in 'Who killed Cock Robin?' sold the victim's car 'to a man from Haddenham'.

Haddenham morris men performing at Christ Church College, Oxford. They also performed on Haddenham Church End Green in 'Judgement Day'.

Real Aylesbury ducks in a row.

Haddenham Barn.   *Haddenham Methodist Church, the largest Witchert building in the world.*

Long Crendon

'Needles and lace'

Crendon's High Street is a treasure trove of history and picturesque cottages and houses. English Heritage lists nearly 100 properties in the village.

The High Street is also long, hence the addition of 'Long' to the village's name, presumably to avoid confusion with the nearby village of Grendon, which nowadays has a high security prison. Not that this was the reason for clarification, the 'Long' was added during the English Civil War, long (no pun intended) before the prison was built.

The High Street encompasses the whole life of the village, starting at one end with the parish church and finishing at the other with the Churchill Arms. In between is the old Court House, the Eight Bells, old needle makers' cottages, a medieval farmhouse, shops and a chapel. It also has the benefit of effectively being a cul de sac to through traffic and still has a nineteenth-century look about it, a fact very much appreciated by the producers of *Midsomer Murders*.

Across the main Thame to Bicester road, which divides the High Street from the rest of the village, is a Tudor manor house, a *Midsomer Murders* regular. It can be viewed through its archway off Frogmore Lane.

Needle making started in the village around the sixteenth century (one of only two places in England, the other being Aylesbury, where needles were manufactured). However, the advent of the Industrial Revolution saw the needle making move to Redditch. Needle workers' cottages can be seen at 7–9 High Street and the Old Needle House, a needle factory dating back to the early nineteenth century, can be seen at 23 Chilton Road.

As with many Buckinghamshire villages, the women and girls of Long Crendon made lace but this, too, suffered at the expense of the Industrial Revolution, almost being driven to extinction by machine-made lace.

Opposite page: Long Crendon Manor appeared in 'Garden of Death', 'The Axeman Cometh' and was a Spiritualist church in 'Things that Go Bump'.

Right. Top to bottom: The Mound, Long Crendon; Long Crendon Court House and church featured in 'Dead Letters' and 'Blood Wedding'; Eight Bells Inn, Long Crendon, was the Florey Arms in 'Blood on the Saddle' and also appeared in 'The Oblong Murders' and 'A Tale of Two Hamlets'; Long Crendon Church Green.

Waddesdon Manor was used fleetingly, well at least the café was, as a French brasserie in 'Death of a Stranger'! The Barnaby family, on holiday in France, had a meal there.

WADDESDON

'Not a bush to be seen, nor a bird to be heard'

Waddesdon village, straddling the A41 5 miles west of Aylesbury, is an ancient agricultural community dating from Saxon times. Little had changed over the centuries until in 1874 the Duke of Marlborough sold 2,700 acres of clay farmland around the village to Baron Ferdinand de Rothschild, High Sheriff of Buckinghamshire, Liberal MP for Aylesbury and, most importantly, a member of the wealthy Rothschild banking family. At that point, Waddesdon effectively became an estate village.

'Not a bush to be seen, nor a bird to be heard', was Baron Ferdinand's remark on his first sight of Lodge Hill with its wonderful views over the Aylesbury Vale. This was where he proposed to build Waddesdon Manor House.

The manor house was designed in the Renaissance style of a sixteenth-century French château and was built as a family home as well as a house for the baron's extensive collection of art, tapestries and furniture.

By 1880 the baron had reshaped the clay farmland landscape with mature trees surrounding his new house. An aviary was added in 1889. In 1900 one of the largest glasshouses in Britain was built to provide flowers for the house and soft fruit for the dinner table. Prize-winning orchids were also grown in it.

Waddesdon Manor was given to the National Trust on the death of James de Rothschild in 1957. It is now a popular tourist attraction, with a world-renowned collection of French furniture, paintings and decorative arts, extensive gardens, a superb wine cellar and a Rococo-style aviary. It has the obligatory garden centre, called a 'plant centre', children's corner, restaurants and gift shops.

As for the village, it is still dominated by buildings constructed by the Rothschild family, the Five Arrows Hotel, the Village Hall, and the houses built for the manor employees. All bear the coat of arms of the Rothschilds, a clenched fist holding five arrows surrounded by the family motto, *Concordia, Integritas, Industria* (Harmony, Integrity, Industry). The coat of arms, 'like arrows in the hands of a warrior' (Psalm 127), symbolises the five sons of Mayer Rothschild, founder of the dynasty, who sent them to Austria, England, France, Germany and Italy to expand the Rothschild business empire.

Right. Bottom left: Waddesdon Manor aviary; Bottom right: Annual Waddesdon Manor horse event.

Above left: Waddesdon Five Arrows Hotel.

Above: The Five Arrows depicted on a balcony at Waddesdon Manor.

THE RIDGEWAY NATIONAL TRAIL

THE RIDGEWAY PATH

'Britain's oldest highway'

The Chilterns are criss-crossed by ancient and modern byways and highways: the Roman roads, Icknield Way and Akeman Street; the Grand Union Canal, the trunk route of Britain's canal network; the seventeenth-, eighteenth- and nineteenth-century turnpike roads; the railway lines from London Paddington, London Marylebone and London Euston; the M40 motorway; the future high-speed rail route; and England's oldest road, the Ridgeway.

The Ridgeway National Trail is one of England's oldest roads. It is 87.30 miles long, according to an official signpost near Ivinghoe Beacon, and follows much of the ancient chalk ridge route used by prehistoric man.

For at least 5,000 years travellers, merchants, herdsmen and fighting men have used the Ridgeway. Originally connecting the east coast of England to the south west coast in Dorset, the Ridgeway provided a reliable trading route, the high, dry ground making travel easy and providing a measure of protection by giving travellers a commanding view and a warning against potential attacks. It was probably as important to prehistoric man as the M40 is to twenty-first-century man. The years 3000 BC and AD 2000 meet at the bottom of Stokenchurch cutting where the M40 crosses over the Ridgeway.

Opposite page: Ivinghoe Beacon, the eastern end of the Ridgeway.

Top right: 3000 BC meets AD 2000 as the M40 motorway crosses over the Ridgeway.

Bottom right: The glorious green Ridgeway.

BLEDLOW

Like Dinton, Bledlow-cum-Saunderton is a large rural parish comprising several hamlets. Within its boundary lie the hamlets of Bledlow, Bledlow Ridge, Forty Green (not the one near Beaconsfield which appears in several episodes of *Midsomer Murders*, well at least the Royal Standard of England country pub does!), Pitch Green, Rout's Green, Skittle Green, Holly Green and, naturally, part of Saunderton.

Bledlow is the most western of the hamlets, which all stand on the northern spur of the Chilterns. It is positioned just above the low-lying meadows that stretch across the Thame Valley to Haddenham. Above Bledlow, on the north slope of Wain Hill, is the Bledlow Cross, cut in the turf, and visible for miles.

Bledlow Church stands in a splendid position overlooking the Aylesbury Vale and is built to an unusual plan. There are two aisles.

Close to the east end of the church is a steep wooded combe called the Lyde. The nearness of the church to the steep banks of the combe has inspired a local saying:

'They that live and do abide, shall see Bledlow Church fall into the Lyde.'

'They that live and do abide,
shall see Bledlow Church fall into the Lyde.'

So much for the reliability of local sayings as this disaster does not seem very imminent.

Several springs emerge from the chalk in the combe and form a small pool. The brook running from the pool is called the Lyde Brook and it was used by two paper mills, Bledlow Mill and North Mill.

Unfortunately, as 'Inspector Barnaby' was not around in Victorian times, there is still the unsolved mystery of the Bledlow Ridge Murder. On the evening of 28 September 1893, John Kingham of Bledlow was murdered in Yewsden wood. The next day PC Henry Ware found his body in the wood, with his skull battered in from behind and his throat cut. No one has been found guilty of the crime. 'Who dunnit?'

Lions of Bledlow Inn disguised as 'The Queens Arms' in 'Dead Man's 11' or even 'The Dog and Partridge' in 'King's Crystal'.

'Badgers Drift' Church, better known as Bledlow Church.

CADSDEN

'Cherry Pie and the Cats'

Cadsden, as I am reliably assured by a resident, means 'The Cats' Den'. In the eighteenth century, excise men, the 'Cats', as they were nicknamed, were stationed in the area to catch contraband traffic, which was known to pass through the hamlet. Not having any official lodgings, the 'Cats' improvised their own, the cats' den.

Trade, contraband or not, has from time immemorial always passed through the area. The Ridgeway is literally on the doorstep of Cadsden, passing straight through the hamlet, and the Plough Inn is probably the only inn in the country whose street address is, rightfully, The Ridgeway.

The inn, nestling in a clearing in the wooded foothills of the Chilterns and dating back to the sixteenth century, is worth the visit to Cadsden. Originally it was a staging post for the stagecoaches travelling from Thame to London. They probably stopped at the inn to pick up an extra two horses to get the stagecoach up and over Longdown Hill on the way to Great Missenden.

A visit to the Plough Inn could have you seeing some recognisable faces. The Prime Minister's country residence, Chequers, is the first property to be encountered along the Ridgeway walking north-east from Cadsden. Rumours that PM's have been seen quaffing a drink in the Plough are definitely true.

Over 100 years ago the tradition of celebrating the end of the local cherry season with a festival started. In recent years the Cherry Pie Festival has been revived and is held on the first Sunday in August at the Plough Inn.

Cadsden is one of the few locations in *Midsomer Murders* that retains, well almost, its identity. Its 'Midsomer' name is 'Cadsden Ridge'.

Top right: The Ridgeway at Cadsden.

Bottom right: The Plough Inn, Cadsden, featured in 'Down among the Dead Men'.

WATLINGTON

There are many towns and villages in the area that proudly proclaim they are the largest, most beautiful and any other superlative adjective place in the world. Watlington, on the other hand, is reputedly England's smallest market town. What is more, it no longer has a market, although I have seen the twenty-first-century mobile fishmonger parked in the old market area next to the town's excellent butchers.

In the centre of Watlington is its Grade II listed Town Hall, built in 1664 by Thomas Stonor, of Stonor Manor, to commemorate the restoration of the monarchy at the end of the Civil War. Originally the Hall had three uses: market house, school and meeting place. Nowadays it is administered by a Town Hall Charity Trustee and is available for hire at £7 per hour. The undercroft, the street level open area under the Town Hall where the market was held, can also be rented at £7 per hour. No doubt the mobile fishmonger takes advantage of this bargain offer.

Watlington has a very rural character, nestling in the shadows of the Chiltern Hills, with rolling countryside dotted with farms, hidden valleys, sleepy villages and medieval hamlets. It is ideal for walking, with a wonderful network of rights of way, including the Ridgeway. Go off the beaten track and discover such gems as Swyncombe with its historic church, the sleepy hamlet of Cookley Green and Christmas Common with its magnificent views over the Oxford Plain. Please ignore the sight of Didcot Power Station.

This is also the perfect place to watch red kites soaring overhead – but beware, stories are circulating around Watlington that schoolchildren's lunches are becoming a better option for the red kites than a dead mouse hidden in the undergrowth.

Left to right: Mobile fishmonger, Watlington Town Hall; Watlington Town Hall was seen in 'Judgement Day'; Watlington Butchers; unusually for a Midsomer Murders production, it was retained as a butchers shop in the 'Judgement Day' episode

LEWKNOR

The small and quiet village of Lewknor lies at the foot of the Chiltern Hills, close to the ancient Ridgeway and the more recent M40 motorway as it emerges from the massive cutting through the Chiltern chalk at Stokenchurch. The building of the motorway and the resultant rerouting of the Watlington–Risborough road around the southern side of the village effectively made the village a cul de sac at its eastern end.

Until the last century the village residents were mainly agricultural labourers, who worked on local farms. To serve the farms the village had a blacksmith, a farm equipment supplier and repairer and a garage with petrol pumps.

There were originally two inns in the village. Now the only one is the Leathern Bottel, a sixteenth-century timber-framed building with brick filling and a reputation for good food and ales.

The school featured in *Midsomer Murders* is mainly thatched and was built in 1836 on the site of some old cottages. The vicar persuaded All Souls College, Oxford, which owns most of the village, to pay for the demolition of the cottages and the building of the school.

A spring flows from near the church to join the River Thame and was, in the past, the main source of village water. The village washerwomen, so they say, required help to fetch forty buckets of water from the spring every day for the villagers' laundering.

Lewknor cut off at the eastern end by the M40, ideal for filming 'Death and Dust', 'The House in the Woods' and 'A Tale of Two Hamlets'.

Lewknor School was used as the Upper Warden police quarters in 'A Tale of Two Hamlets'.

ALONG THE OXFORDSHIRE MOTORWAY

GREAT AND LITTLE HASELEY

'The most influential English gardener'

The Haseleys take you back a few centuries; many of the houses date back to the early seventeenth century. However, it was an American-born socialite, Nancy Lancaster, that put the Haseleys on the map.

In 1954 Nancy Lancaster bought Haseley Court, an eighteenth-century house, in Little Haseley, which she saved from ruin, as well as flying the Confederate flag over the house. She is specially remembered for recreating the 10-acre garden with imagination and style. The British interior designer David Hicks called Nancy Lancaster 'the most influential English gardener'.

However, garden design was not her only forté. Her influence on furnishing and decoration in Britain was immeasurable.

Opposite page: The M40 sweeping through Oxfordshire's 'Midsomer'.

Top right: Great Haseley Church, seen in a funeral in 'Dark Autumns' and a wedding in 'Midsomer Rhapsody'.

Bottom right: The entrance gate, Haseley Court, Little Haseley, featured in 'Who killed Cock Robin?'.

THAME

'England's greatest one-day agricultural show'

Thame is a traditional English market town at its best and the *Midsomer Murders* production team loves it. I have enjoyed the town for over fifty years. When I first went there, the wide upper High Street, where the market is held, was cobbled. It had a railway station with a superb Isambard Kingdom Brunel–designed train station and a steam train service between Princes Risborough and Oxford. It now shares a modern railway station, Haddenham and Thame Parkway, in the village of Haddenham some 3 miles away.

The right to hold the weekly street market was granted by Royal Charter in the twelfth century and the large general market is still held every Tuesday. There is also a regular livestock market on Tuesdays, Wednesdays and Fridays and farmers markets on the second Tuesday and the fifth Saturday in a month.

Originally the only building in the centre of the town was its oldest inn, the Birdcage, reputedly haunted. Over the years, buildings such as the Town Hall have been erected around it. Despite this, and with the centre being a dedicated conservation area, there is, almost, a complete absence of modern buildings – an architectural historian's delight, going back to the thirteenth century.

A visit to the Information Centre in the Town Hall for copies of three circular walks around the town will be very beneficial. Then you can set out and discover the historic hidden gems of Thame for yourself.

Top left: Thame's oldest inn, The Birdcage.

Bottom left: Cornmarket, Thame, a very popular street, which appears in numerous Midsomer Murders *episodes.*

Bottom right: Thame Market with the 'Midsomer Life' offices in the background, also used as 'Causton Library' in 'Vixen's Run'.

Thame hosts England's greatest one-day agricultural show, the Oxfordshire County and Thame Show, dating back over 130 years. It is a traditional show featuring livestock and horse classes, a dog show, show jumping, vintage vehicles, trade stands, craft tents and a large food marquee. Originally held in September, it now takes place on the last Saturday in July. A great family day out that I have regularly enjoyed.

Until its date change, the show took place at the same time as the ancient Thame hiring fair. A hiring fair in medieval times was, as the name indicates, the local employment exchange where workers and employers met to arrange next year's annual employment agreement. The fair nowadays is an enormous funfair that closes the centre of the town. A smaller funfair, often referred to as the firing fair, probably for obvious reasons, is held around Michaelmas Day at the beginning of October.

One of those delightful historical English folk stories, which no one can prove or disprove, relates that William Shakespeare visited Thame High Street during his time as a strolling player. There is, however, one story we do know is true. Henry VIII and Catherine Howard came to Thame during their honeymoon, staying at the residence of Lord Williams of Thame, Rycote Palace.

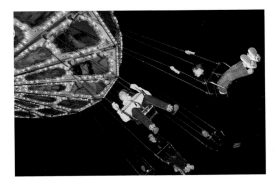

Top left: The annual Oxfordshire County and Thame Show.

Middle left: Spread Eagle Inn, the 'Moorcroft Hotel' in 'Midsomer Life'.

Top right: The Thame High Street entrance to the original sixteenth-century grammar school.

Middle right: A chocolate shop in Thame, or Madrigal's old camera shop in 'Picture of Innocence'.

Bottom right: Thame Town Hall, also known as 'Causton Town Hall'.

A view from Headington Hill of the Oxford Spires.

OXFORD

Oxford is Oxford in the real world as well as the fictional world of *Midsomer Murders*. So much has been written about the city, the university, the colleges and its famous graduates that any words of mine would add nothing to the story of Oxford. However, Oxford has one feature, owned by the university, which is overlooked and greatly underrated by the tourists: the Botanic Gardens.

The gardens comprise a walled garden, the home to the Gardens' oldest tree, an English yew, and the glasshouses, which allow the cultivation of plants needing protection from the extremes of British weather.

There has been a glasshouse at the Botanic Garden for over 300 years. The first house was built in 1675 from stone, with a slate roof and small windows. Seventeenth-century gardeners did not yet realise that plants needed light in order to grow. Since then horticulture has moved on. Now, plants from all over the world are grown within a small area enabling visitors to experience the diversity of the plant kingdom.

There are seven glasshouses for plants from dry deserts to tropical rainforests:
– The Alpine House where plants from mountainous regions of the world are grown.
– The Fernery. There are over 8,400 species of ferns in the world and the plants in this house show just how many shades of green there are.
– The Lily House is home to the oldest part of the glasshouses. Marvel at the large round 'pie dish'-like leaves of the Victoria cruziana lily.
– The Insectivorous House where plants from marshes and swamps from around the world thrive. See the plants that trap and digest small insects.
– The Arid House. In the centre of the house are the larger cacti and succulents.
– The Orchid House, as seen in the *Midsomer Murders* episode 'Orchis Fatalis'.
– The Palm House. The largest glasshouse in the garden, this house grows palms, citrus fruits, peppers, sweet potatoes and pawpaws.

Oxford Botanic Gardens, greenhouses and the River Cherwell: scene of a chase in 'Orchis Fatalis'.

Oxford Botanic Gardens – an obvious choice for 'Orchis Fatalis'.

Oxford Botanic Gardens and Magdalen College tower.

Red Kites and the Vicar of Dibley

Red Kites

'The greatest conservation success story of the twentieth century'

Gliding on thermals rising from the chalk escarpment, the red kite, a spectacular bird of prey, has become a common and well-loved everyday sight in the Chilterns, but only in the past twenty years.

Red kites had been driven to extinction in England by human persecution at the end of the nineteenth century. Between 1989 and 1994, red kites from Spain were imported and released into the Chilterns at Wormsley Park by the RSPB and English Nature with the kind permission of Sir Paul Getty, owner of the Wormsley Park Estate. They started breeding in 1992 and now there are over 300 breeding pairs in the area.

The magnificent red kite, distinguished by its russet red plumage, 2m wingspan, forked tail and its eyes constantly looking downwards in search of prey, can best be seen, soaring overhead, in the Aston Rowant National Nature Reserve, near Watlington. The reserve is perched high on the Chilterns escarpment with fantastic views over the Oxford Plain and the Aylesbury Vale. The reserve is a mixture of woodland, juniper scrub and chalk grassland, which in summer has an abundance of wildflowers, bees and butterflies.

Other places to see the red kites are: Watlington Hill (Oxfordshire), Stokenchurch (Buckinghamshire), Chinnor (Oxfordshire) and West Wycombe Hill (Buckinghamshire).

Opposite page: Bird's-eye view of a red kite gliding along the Hambleden Brook Valley.

Storm over Wormsley Park Cricket Ground, setting of a cricket match in 'Secrets and Spies'.

WORMSLEY PARK

'The most beautiful cricket ground in England'

Wormsley Park is a 2,500-acre estate with an eighteenth-century country house and the most beautiful cricket ground in England, Sir Paul Getty's Ground. It is now the private home of Mark Getty and his family, the son of the late American-British billionaire philanthropist, Sir Paul Getty.

Sir Paul Getty was a devotee of all things English, especially the most English of games, cricket. His vision and creation of a cricket ground at Wormsley was a source of joy to him, his family and every cricket lover who has ever watched or played cricket there. I will never forget my first visit.

Wormsley has rightly been described as the most beautiful ground in England. A red telephone box sits next to the thatched pavilion, overlooking the immaculate playing area, with a backdrop of the sloping Chiltern Hills and red kites floating overhead on air currents as the game is played beneath them. The two ends of the ground are known as 'The Deer Park End' and 'The Dibley End'. The latter is named after the village of Turville, better known as 'Dibley' in the television series *The Vicar of Dibley*, which lies at the bottom of the valley sloping down from the ground.

STONOR MANOR

'Possibly the most beautiful setting for any house in England'

Situated in a most beautiful setting, Stonor is one of England's oldest manor houses. It has been owned by the same family, the Catholic Stonor family, for over 850 years, defying King Henry VIII, the Protestant Reformation and revolution.

The house has a fine collection of family portraits, stained glass, Old Master drawings, European bronzes and modern ceramics from England, Denmark, Korea and Japan.

Outside are a walled Italianate garden and the former kitchen garden, which has spectacular views of the Chilterns.

In the undulating slopes of the estate grounds, a herd of fallow deer graze, whilst overhead the red kites and buzzards glide on the rising thermals.

Afterwards enjoy a good cup of English tea in the Tea Room.

Thatched scoreboard, Wormsley Park.

Stonor House and the village of Stonor have featured in many episodes of Midsomer Murders.

TURVILLE

'Dibley'

Lying peacefully in the steep-sided valley of the Hambleden Brook (dry as I write this) Turville, if you ignore the 4x4 vehicles and the metalled road, takes you back a century or maybe two. Seemingly isolated from the modern world, it is but a few miles from the M40, High Wycombe and Henley-on-Thames.

This unique location has brought the television and filmmakers to Turville on many occasions. It is 'Dibley' in *The Vicar of Dibley*. The church of St Mary the Virgin is the 'Dibley' parish church of 'St Barnabas'.

The impressive Cobstone Windmill, which looks like a white smock, stands high, overlooking the valley. It gained fame, as well as a complete makeover, when it was used in the film *Chitty Chitty Bang Bang*.

The local pub, the Bull and Butcher, 'The Chalk and Gown' in 'Midsomer Parva', is popular with 'DCI Barnaby' and 'DS Hughes'. Its popularity with the filmmakers has not gone unnoticed by the landlord. The menu offers Midsomer Burgers and Chitty Chitty Bangers and Mash. I enjoyed the visit.

Top left: Turville, seen in 'Straw Woman', whilst schoolboys in 'Murder on St Malley's Day' slipped into the Bull and Butcher.

Bottom left: Cobstone Mill, Ibstone, also known as 'Chitty Chitty Bang Bang Mill' and seen in 'Dark Autumns'.

Left: Bull and Butcher, Turville.

NETTLEBED

Nettlebed is not a village you would pass through and say, 'I must stop here', until you see, in the middle of a modern housing estate, a large bottle kiln. Curiosity makes you investigate.

The village and nearby Crocker End are set in the middle of wooded countryside, a large area of common land, on the top of a rich bed of clay and with a plentiful supply of firewood and spring water. The two villages were a natural site for brick and pottery making and played an important part in the history of brick making. It was the most important brick and tile-making centre in the Chilterns from the mid-fourteenth century onwards. Records show that the first bricks were made by a settlement of Flemish brick makers. They supplied bricks and tiles for the building of Wallingford Castle and Stonor Manor. This gives an indication of the size of the operation, as both theses buildings would have needed hundreds of thousands of bricks and tiles.

'The Flemings and Flemish Bricks'

The bottle kiln in the village is the only one of its type preserved in the country. It was built around 1700 and was in use up until 1938, in later years being converted to a lime-burning kiln.

In 1902, Robert Fleming bought 2,000 acres of land, kilns, clayworks and cottages in the village, the beginning of the Fleming family's involvement with Nettlebed. Today the current members of the family live locally, run the estate and take an active part in village life. However, most people only know of the family through the writings of one of Robert's grandsons, Ian, the author of the *James Bond* books.

The White Hart Inn replaced the George Inn, Dorchester, in the 'Maid of Splendour', when the 'Maid' was given a makeover.

Left: White Hart Inn, Nettlebed, the 'Maid of Splendour' after her makeover.

Right: The surviving brick kiln, Nettlebed.

Pooh Sticks Bridge, scene of the World Pooh Sticks Championships.

POOH STICKS, CLUMPS AND AN ABBEY

The World Pooh Sticks Championships are held every March at Little Wittenham Bridge, a short way downstream from Days Lock on the River Thames. The bridge spans the river in two sections with the villages of Little Wittenham on one side and Dorchester on the other. The event owes its beginning to former lock-keeper Lynn David who noticed walkers throwing sticks in the river and rushing to the other side of the bridge to see whose stick emerged first. They were, of course, imitating the game created and made famous by Pooh Bear and his friends. This gave Lynn the idea of creating an event to raise funds for the RNLI.

Pooh Sticks of a different type, namely a dead body, floated under the bridge in *Midsomer Murders*' 'Dark Secrets', which, rather humorously, was called by television critics 'Death by *Daily Telegraph*'. Watch it again and you will know why.

BRIGHTWELL BALDWIN   *'Relaxed dining'*

Brightwell Baldwin is a very small, one country lane village. It has a church, so I cannot call it a hamlet, and a typical old English inn, the Lord Nelson. The inn has a first class restaurant, the only way a small village inn can survive these days, and, of course, a history. No doubt originally a thatched cottage with later additions to the original stone building including a quaint veranda, which would not be out of place in Charleston, South Carolina. In 1905, following complaints from the church and the local squire that the local estate workers had been overdoing it on the scrumpy, the inn was closed and became a shop, a post office and finally a private house. However, in 1971 a passing couple liked the look of it. They decided to restore the inn to its former glory and reopened it on 21 October 1971, Trafalgar Day.

Full of fresh flowers, lit candles and a splendid inglenook fireplace, the Lord Nelson provides a perfect atmosphere for relaxing and dining.

BRITWELL SALOME   *'The Goose was cooked'*

'It comes as no surprise to learn that Britwell Salome is a location for 'Midsomer Murders'. Today, though, this pretty Chilterns village of 200 people has its own real-life mystery: the case of the disappearing chefs.'

The Times, *13 February 2010*

Britwell Salome had a public house, The Goose, which had been awarded a Michelin Star in January 2010 for the third time. Sadly, it was not a business success and it closed.

However, Britwell Salome is still worth a detour to drive down Britwell Hill. It drops dead straight for half a mile from one of the highest points in the Chilterns, over 700ft above sea level, providing spectacular views over the Thames Valley and Oxfordshire. It then crosses the Ridgeway before curving north and continuing straight for another mile into the village. Locally it is known as 'Chitty Chitty Bang Bang Hill'.

Red kites are commonly seen and Britwell House (featured in *Midsomer Murders*) is clearly seen on the left as you descend the hill.

Britwell Salome House featured in 'Birds of Pray' and 'Death in Chorus'.

Dorchester-on-Thames from Wittenham Clumps.

DORCHESTER-ON-THAMES

'Cradle of English Christianity'

Dorchester is a charming riverside Oxfordshire village lying at the confluence of the Rivers Thame and Thames. The nature reserve of the imposing Sinodun Hills (locally known as Wittenham clumps), which overlooks the village, provides great opportunities for outdoor activities and offers commanding views over the River Thames and Oxfordshire countryside. To the south-east are the Chilterns and to the south-west the Berkshire Downs.

Dorchester is steeped in history. An Iron Age hill fort existed on the Sinodun Hills. It was a Celtic market centre and a Roman town, but it was the advent of Christianity that put Dorchester-on-Thames on the map. In AD 634 the Pope decided that the Saxons of the Thames Valley needed to be converted to Christianity. He created a new diocese under a Bishop of Dorchester and by default Dorchester became the capital of Wessex.

Dorchester Abbey was built and enlarged over several centuries but in 1536 King Henry VIII dissolved the abbey. Dorchester became a small village with a huge church, the abbey church of St Peter and St Paul.

Today, the superb medieval abbey church dominates the delightful setting of timbered houses, thatched cottages and ancient inns. Within the abbey confines are the Abbey Guesthouse, housing an interesting museum, gift shop and tearoom, and the attractive Cloister Gardens and Cloister Gallery.

An imposing Victorian lychgate connects the abbey grounds to the High Street with a variety of outstanding period buildings. Many date back to the seventeenth and eighteenth centuries when Dorchester was an important stagecoach stop between London and Oxford. There were no fewer than ten inns here in the eighteenth century and two notable coaching inns, the George and the White Hart. Today, both retain much of their old architecture and character.

Such a large number of inns is not a reflection on the drinking habits of the townspeople of Dorchester, it is more an indication of the number of travellers who passed through the town in the eighteenth century. An inn was originally a house providing accommodation, food, and drink, especially for travellers.

Dorchester Abbey through the lychgate, with the tea rooms and museum on the left, featured in 'The House in the Woods',

The George Inn, Dorchester, the 'Maid of Splendour' before she had a makeover and moved to The White Hart, Nettlebed.

Ewelme from Rabbit Hill. Take a photograph from the spot where many film and TV cameramen have stood. Seen in 'Beyond the Grave', 'The Black Book', 'Small Mercies' and 'The Sword of Guillaume'.

EWELME
'Quiet waters'

To find Ewelme you have a winding country lane drive with helicopters hovering over you. I would think the helicopters must be a nightmare for television and film producers. The reason: to the west of the village is RAF Benson, home to several Royal Air Force helicopter squadrons.

The airfield is a well-known frost hollow, often recording the coldest temperatures in the UK, as low as minus 17°C in recent times. Whereas in the village of Ewelme the rapidly flowing Ewelme Brook, which starts in a spring just north of the village, has a constant temperature of plus 10°C, ideal for the growing of watercress. The village and the watercress beds run side by side creating a long and straggling linear village. Due to legislation, production of watercress on a commercial basis in the village ceased in the twentieth century.

The village has a set of fifteenth-century cloistered almshouses officially called 'The Two Chaplains and Thirteen Poor Men of Ewelme in the County of Oxford'. If you count the almshouses there are now only eight of the original thirteen.

Ewelme School is old. In fact it is believed to be the oldest state school in the UK, also dating from the fifteenth century.

The finest view of the village can be seen from Rabbits Hill. There is room to park a car and then you can take a photograph from the same spot where many television and film cameras have rolled.

Left: Water cress stream, Ewelme.

Above: Wild watercress, Ewelme.

WARBOROUGH

'One of the largest village greens'

If there was a competition for the village with all the amenities required for a 'Midsomer Murder', Warborough would be a strong contender.

It has a twelfth-century church, a vicarage, a seventeenth-century manor house, a memorial hall, a village inn, a village shop, a village school, a village green, thatched cottages, half-timbered houses, a Women's Institute, cricket and football clubs, a summer fête, allotments, farms, fields, woods and the River Thames. No wonder it has appeared in so many *Midsomer Murders*.

Warborough Green is one of the finest and possibly the largest village green in Oxfordshire. The edge of the green has sycamore, lime, oak and horse chestnut trees, and on the north and south sides attractive residential properties. The Six Bells Inn is on the south-west corner.

On Sundays in summer, cricket is played on the green. There is no better village green in Oxfordshire for pleasurably passing an afternoon away.

The annual Warborough Summer Fayre with a pig roast, silver band, classic cars, games, cream teas, raffle, crafts and much, much, more, would be credit to any 'Midsomer' village fête.

Warborough Cricket Club Pavilion: 'Badger's Drift' village hall in the 'Great and the Good'.

Right: The Six Bells Inn, Warborough, also known as 'The Luck in the World', the 'Quill Inn' and the 'Black Swan'.

The 'Four Feathers Hotel' in 'Market for Murder', also seen in 'Tainted Fruit' and 'The Sword of Guillaume'.

WALLINGFORD

Wallingford is not the prettiest market town but it is the best-preserved example of a Saxon town in England. Unlike the nearby market town of Thame with its wide main street, Wallingford is cramped and a traffic nightmare where the High Street crosses Castle and St Martin's Streets. However, it oozes history and modern-day motorists should remember that King Alfred the Great built the town to defend himself from Viking raiders and not to cater for a Mini, 1,000 years later. Modern-day planners have catered for the car with a by-pass, parking by the river, a campsite and, if you come by river, new mooring facilities. Enjoy the stroll over the beautiful 300-yard-long bridge that spans the River Thames, along the High Street and into the town centre. The five-minute stroll will take you past antique shops and cafés into Wallingford's bustling market square.

William the Conqueror crossed the river at this point in 1066, no doubt when he decided to build a castle at Wallingford. The castle lasted as a royal residence until the time of the Black Death and was demolished by the order of Oliver Cromwell in 1646 after a sixty-five-day siege. Take a pleasant walk to Castle Gardens and see the remains of the castle.

The Corn Exchange in the market place is now a theatre managed by the local drama group, The Sinodun Players. Agatha Christie, who lived and is buried in Cholsey, on the outskirts of Wallingford, was once their president. And that nicely brings us to the 'Midsomer Players', who also used the Corn Exchange in several episodes of *Midsomer Murders*.

Wallingford Museum, a delightful local history museum, follows on the crime theme with an Agatha Christie section and one investigating the town's darker past. The main attraction of a visit to the museum is 'The Wallingford Story', a sight and sound telling of the history of Wallingford through the ages.

Lovers of steam trains and nostalgia will enjoy the Cholsey and Wallingford Railway, locally known as the Bunk.

Bad weather over the Wallingford Bridge.

Wallingford Theatre, also known as 'Causton Playhouse'.

The Henley Royal Regatta, a glimpse of which can be seen in 'Dead in the Water'.

PORT, PIMMS AND WINE

HENLEY-ON-THAMES

'A town inextricably linked with the River Thames'

Henley and Thames go together like a horse and carriage.

The origins of the town owe much to its location on the river and its development as a port. In the sixteenth century, historian William Camden described the majority of inhabitants as bargemen carrying wood and corn to London by water. Nowadays, the only bargemen are holidaymakers, in converted old canal barges, slowly wending their way down the Oxford Canal from the Midlands, to enjoy the pleasures of gently cruising down the Thames through the beautiful English countryside.

Despite the demise of the river as a waterway for commercial traffic, the Thames still maintains its importance to the prosperity of the town. One word sums this up – rowing.

Now 'all play and no work' for the old canal barges.

Henley town centre.

Henley-on-Thames is the world-renowned centre for rowing. Each summer, during the week after the Wimbledon Tennis Championships, the Henley Royal Regatta is held on 'Henley Reach', a stretch of the river from Temple Island to the Henley Bridge, 1 mile, 550 yards long and naturally straight.

The Regatta is a great hospitality event with marquees lining both sides of the river. Inside the marquees, companies entertain their clients to champagne lunches, afternoon teas and Pimms. Occasionally the guests will wander outside to watch a race, especially if their old school or university is competing.

Visitors can enjoy a boat trip on the Regatta course, either in one of the commercial boats that operate along the stretch or under their own steam in a rowing boat.

The Thames would not be the same without Mr Toad, Ratty, Badger and Mole. See then all at the *Wind in the Willows* exhibition in Henley's award-winning River and Rowing Museum.

Left: The umpires, Henley Royal Regatta.

MARLOW

'The Nymph that Mourns a Famous American'

Marlow is one of my favourite towns in Buckinghamshire, possibly *the* favourite. Its setting, nestling on the Buckinghamshire bank of the River Thames, with a little white suspension bridge connecting the wide High Street with the Berkshire bank, is beautiful. The town's wide High Street is a shopper's delight and, these days, a coffee drinker's delight also.

As you cross the river and enter Marlow from the Berkshire side you pass the church and come to a little green with a French milestone, the French connection again, and a statue. It is a charming stone figure of a young girl. The statue is elegant and graceful. Around the pedestal are inscribed the words:

> *For it is not right that in a house*
> *The Muses haunt morning should dwell;*
> *Such things befit us not.*
> *In Happy Memory of Charles Frohman, 1860-1915*

Who was Charles Frohman? An American impresario, who came to England in 1893, acquired the lease of the Duke of York's and Globe Theatres in London. He met J.M. Barrie, a young playwright, liked his new play, *Peter Pan*, decided to produce it at the Duke of York's Theatre and the rest is history. His connection with Marlow? To escape the hustle and bustle of the London theatrical business world he would come and stay in green and tranquil Marlow. Sadly he was on board the *Lusitania* when the liner was torpedoed by the Germans in the First World War and was reported 'lost at sea'.

Far right: The nymph statue, Marlow.

Hambleden Locks featured in 'The Animal Within'.

HAMBLEDEN

I have used the description 'prettiest' about numerous villages in the Chilterns. This is the amazing reality of the Chilterns. It really is an area of outstanding natural and manmade beauty.

Hambleden is another of those pretty Chiltern villages, in one of the most attractive Chiltern valleys, the now dry Hambleden Brook valley.

Hambleden, surprisingly, still has a village post office and shop with a welcoming café. There you can stop, sit down and have something to eat and drink.

A little-known fact about the village is that it was a base for American soldiers during the build up to D-Day in 1944. What I find most interesting about this is that the US magazine *LIFE* sent photographer Frank Scherschel to capture lesser-known scenes of the Second World War: American troops training in a small English village, Hambleden. Even more amazing is that Scherschel filmed in colour. His photograph of Coombe Terrace taken on 1 May 1944 could well have been taken today. Only the tree has aged.

'A dry valley and a dry wine'

Hambleden was the home of William Henry Smith, founder of the newsagents and bookseller, W.H. Smith. Another past resident was Lord Cardigan, famous for his role in leading the ill-fated Charge of the Light Brigade, who was born in the flint and stone Manor House. The sea chest that he took to the Crimea can be seen in the church.

A mile to the south of Hambleden, at Mill End on the River Thames, is Hambleden Lock, featured in the novel *Three Men in a Boat*.

A visit to Hambleden must include a detour to the 'Chiltern Valley Winery and Brewery'. The journey is along one of the most picturesque routes in the area. I can assure you that you will not be disappointed with the 'degustation', non-drivers only, when you arrive at your destination.

Looking towards Coombe Terrace, Hambleden.

Post office, shop and café, Hambleden, seen in 'Stranglers Wood' and 'Blood Will Out'.

Cottages, Hambleden, seen in 'Down Among the Dead Men' and 'Who Killed Cock Robin?'.

Three less one men in a boat.

ASTON AND REMENHAM

'Turn around when possible'

Aston and Remenham are a challenge to any sat-nav system. Mine never got me to the Flower Pot Inn, which I believe is in the centre of Aston. Fortunately, I saw a road sign on the Maidenhead to Henley road indicating that Aston was down a narrow high-hedged lane. By the way, it is the only sign for Aston I have ever seen. Several miles down this lane, Aston and the Flower Pot are reached, nestling by the River Thames.

After refreshment, continue along the lane, which follows the river towards Henley, and you come to Remenham, with its pretty flint stone church, which appeared in 'Country Matters'.

HURLEY

'Oldest English Inn or a Modern Coaching Inn?'

Hurley is literally at the end of a lane. Travel any further and you are in the River Thames, but with the knowledge that you are alongside one of its prettiest stretches.

The village has two inns, a relatively young one and an old one, Ye Olde Bell, founded in 1135, which claims to be the oldest in England, as do at least another twenty inns. It became the 'Magna Hotel' in 'They Seek Him Here'.

The younger is a charming sixteenth-century inn, Black Boys, specialising in simply delicious French home cooking. It is so-called after a nickname of Prince Charles, later King Charles II, who had a swarthy complexion and who is said to have visited in secret when fleeing the Roundheads.

Left: Remenham Church, seen in 'Country Matters'.

Right: Ye Olde Bell Inn, Hurley, featured in 'They Seek Him Here'.

Windsor Castle from the River Thames.

A Royal Castle and a Racecourse

Bray

'Pagan fertility symbols, Blooms and a Galaxy of Michelin Stars'

There are many villages that proclaim their success in 'Best Village' and 'Britain in Bloom' competitions by proudly displaying their achievements on large inn post signs, normally on the village green. How times change; when Little Missenden won the 'Best Kept Small Village in Buckinghamshire' award in 1962 it received a small cast-iron plaque that was screwed to a tree. You can easily miss it if you blink.

If there was a village league table for these awards, Bray, in my opinion, would win hands down. I counted over twenty 'Britain in Bloom' awards since 1990. Whatever happened in 1999 – 'null point!'?

And, of course, I must not forget, Bray has more Michelin Stars than any other village in the universe.

So, if you like the very, very best food, this is the village to come to, but you may have to wait over three months for a table. Two of its restaurants, Heston Blumenthal's The Fat Duck and Michel Roux's Waterside Inn, each have three Michelin stars. In 2010 the Waterside Inn became the first restaurant outside France to retain all three stars for twenty-five years.

However, if you are feeling peckish the Hind's Head, a fifteenth-century inn, is the place to go. Lunchtime food is close to perfection. Well, it is owned by Heston Blumenthal!

Visit St Michael's Church and view a rare pagan carving. Enter the churchyard through the attractive lychgate with its lychgate cottages. Inside the church, look up into the rafters near the west door. There you will see a small stone female figure, the Sheela-Na-Gig, who has large breasts and legs spread. She is believed to be a Celtic fertility symbol.

Bray is probably a little too expensive for Midsomer detectives. Consequently only one visit to Bray has been made: the filming, inside St Michael's Church, of the dripping blood scene in 'Ring out your Dead'.

Bray in bloom.

The lychgate, St Michael's Church, Bray.

The Fat Duck restaurant.

The Hinds Head Inn.

The Long Walk, Windsor. Glimpses appear in 'Death in Chorus'.

WINDSOR AND ETON

The castle is worth the journey to Windsor. Words do not do justice to its magnificence, its history, its splendour, its state apartments, St George's Chapel and Queen Mary's dolls house. The impressive tree-lined Long Walk justifies at least one Sunday stroll, but mind the joggers and the low-flying Airbuses and Boeings as they take off from Heathrow Airport.

It was William the Conqueror who started to construct Windsor Castle after his Conquest in 1066. The site was chosen because of its strategic importance, adjacent to the River Thames, which provided convenient and safe travel. In addition, it was close to Windsor Forest, a royal hunting preserve previously used by the Saxon kings, which, one can only assume, was as important.

Prior to its construction, the kings of England went to Brill Castle for relaxation and recreation. However, by the thirteenth century Brill Castle had lost its attraction for the royals. The hunting was excellent in nearby Bernwode Forest but the commute from London must have been too tiring, so they relocated to residences closer to London. Windsor town developed significantly from then on. It is now Royal Windsor with a population of over 30,000. As for Brill, it is still a little hilltop village with an interesting history and a population of just over 1,000, many commuting in the opposite direction to past kings. Nowadays, it is only Sunday afternoon drivers who come to Brill for relaxation and recreation. What a difference patronage makes.

Royal Windsor, one of the most beautiful towns in Berkshire, has another attraction I admire: the Victorian railway station designed with Great Western Railway grandeur for Queen Victoria and built on the doorstep of her castle. It has been beautifully restored as a shopping precinct with a complete set of well-known coffee shops, sandwich bars and restaurants. Remarkably, considering the demise of the railways in the 1960s, now reversed, the real function of the station has not been overlooked. There is still a half-hourly train service to Slough for London.

A walk over the cast-iron bridge from Windsor to Eton High Street follows in the footsteps of 'Inspector Barnaby' and eventually leads to Eton College. The college is famous for Eton Mess, a pudding consisting of a mixture of strawberries, pieces of meringue and cream, the Eton Wall game, an indescribable ball game and, of course its main function, education. Nineteen British Prime Ministers have passed through its classrooms.

If you feel like a flutter on the horses, the Royal Windsor racecourse on the banks of the River Thames has themed flat race meetings every Monday evening in the summer. Arrive in style by boat from Windsor.

Windsor Castle.

Eton High Street, seen in 'The Black Book'.

The locks on the River Thames, close to Windsor Racecourse (seen in the background), featured in 'Bantling Boy'.

The expansive Littlewick Green seen in 'Dead Man's 11', 'A Talent for Life', 'The Animal Within' and 'The Great & The Good'.

LITTLEWICK GREEN

'Sunday afternoon delight'

Littlewick Green is a delight and I can imagine that it was a clearing in the Great Forest of Windsor long before the Normans arrived.

It is set around what seems to be acres of village green, where, for over 200 summers, the glorious sound of leather on willow has been heard. I find it hard to imagine a more idyllic village setting for England's national summer sport. The village public house is naturally called 'The Cricketers' and the village hall acts as the cricket pavilion and scoreboard on summer Sunday afternoons.

The village has one claim to fame. Ivor Novello, composer, singer and actor, lived here. He also used the village hall, doubtless on non-cricketing days, to test out many of his compositions before they were transferred to the West End.

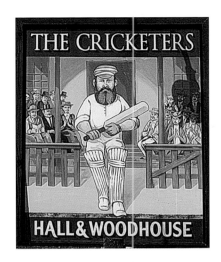

Littlewick Green Village Hall featured in 'Dead Man's 11' and as an antique shop in 'A Talent for Life'.

71

BEECH WOODS AND COMMONS

BURNHAM BEECHES

'England's Ancient Wood'

Historic Burnham Beeches, described as one of the finest woodland tracts anywhere in Britain, is the remnants of a vast forest that once covered almost the entire county of Buckinghamshire. It is owned and managed by the Corporation of London who, in 1880, bought the woodland to save it from prospective developers.

The area is characterised by a diverse mixture of ancient woodland, wood pasture, coppice, ponds and streams, grassland, mire and heathland. The site's most prominent features are the veteran beech and oak pollarded trees, which provide a stable habitat for many rare and endangered deadwood species. The average age of the pollarded trees is estimated to be in excess of 400 years. The largest tree, probably the oldest, is the 'Druid's Oak', believed to be over 800 years old.

The Beeches, located close to Burnham and Beaconsfield, offers many easy walks through its 540 acres of woodland.

Opposite page: Burnham Beeches featured in 'Talking to the Dead'.

BEACONSFIELD

'Ends and PMs'

Midsomer Murders enthusiasts will tell you that Beaconsfield is by far the most used location in the series. They will also tell you that Wallingford is 'Causton', the County Town of 'Midsomer'. My view is that Beaconsfield has done enough to be 'Midsomer's' administration centre.

Beaconsfield, like Amersham, now has a new town, again resulting from the arrival of the railway; this time without protests to my knowledge. The station, situated just under a mile from Old Beaconsfield, became the catalyst for the development of New Beaconsfield with shops and houses.

Contrary the popular belief, Beaconsfield is not the site of a field with a beacon. It is a clearing in a beech wood.

Old Beaconsfield developed around the parish church and a spacious market place at the crossroads of four streets. They were simply named, Aylesbury End, London End, Windsor End and Wycombe End. Congratulations to the aldermen of the town naming roads with simplicity.

A Midsomer Murders cameraman's view: 'A Rare Bird', Slate 233, Take 3.

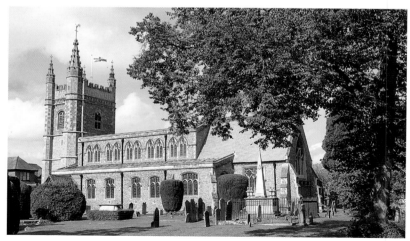

Beaconsfield Church, seen in 'Ghosts of Christmas Past' and 'Four Funerals and a Wedding'.

Old Beaconsfield has a number of old stagecoach inns, as well as some very good restaurants and shops along its wide main street, London and Wycombe Ends. The inns date back to the days when it was a stagecoach stopping point on the road between London and Oxford.

Today the town is very prosperous. It was named 'Britain's richest town' by the *Daily Telegraph* in 2008. It is probably no coincidence that two British Prime Ministers have been associated with the town. One was a winner, Benjamin Disraeli, Conservative Member of Parliament for the town in Victorian times, and one a loser, Tony Blair, the losing Labour candidate for the Beaconsfield constituency in Thatcher times.

New Beaconsfield is the home of Bekonscot model village, the first model village in the world when it opened in 1929. Well worth a visit for parents and grandparents. Oh and children too!

Beaconsfield Bekonscot Model Village, seen in 'Small Matters'.

The Old Tea House, Beaconsfield, where Inspector Barnaby has had the odd cup of tea.

THE RIVER CHESS VALLEY

THE RIVER CHESS

'Meadows, watercress, dragonflies, water voles and kingfishers'

Although it is only a five-minute drive from the M25 motorway, the River Chess's peaceful countryside seems like a world away. It is a classic valley of green undulating hills with cows, sheep and horses grazing in its lush green meadows. Only 11 miles in length from its source near Chesham, it gently meanders its way through flora and fauna-rich water meadows, weirs, a watercress farm and a nature reserve. It supports several protected species, including water vole, kingfisher, stream water crowfoot and brown trout.

Beyond Latimer it flows to the north of Chenies, through Frogmore Meadow, a nature reserve that has probably remained the same for hundreds of years, and then on to Sarratt, the only place on the river where watercress is still grown.

After Sarratt the river turns south to Rickmansworth to become a tributary of the River Colne.

The Chess River Walk, which follows the river, links with the Metropolitan line stations of Chesham, Chorleywood and Rickmansworth, giving visitors the opportunity to walk either part or all of the river valley.

Opposite page: River Chess.

Top right: Chess Valley and the M25.

Bottom right: River Chess.

Chesham Church spire in Church Street seen in 'Written in Blood'.

CHESHAM

Chesham, the largest market town in the Chilterns, nestles amongst beautiful valleys, just south-east of the sources of three chalk streams that converge in the town to form the River Chess. Contrary to popular belief, the town is not named after the river; rather, the river is named after the town.

The prettiest and most interesting part of the town, with its flint stone church, flint stone cottages and the river, is around Church Street. This was the old centre of the town, now separated from the newer town centre by a little by-pass.

In the eighteenth and nineteenth centuries Chesham prospered as a manufacturing town with leather, brush and flag and banner industries, a brewery and three Baptist churches. The boots, brushes and beer have now gone but the banners and the Baptists are still standing proud. Three-quarters of all trade union banners are made in Chesham. Ideal for processional walking, which is fairly appropriate, Chesham is the first 'Walkers are Welcome' town in the Chilterns.

At the end of the Metropolitan Tube line, Chesham is a great place to begin exploring the Chilterns and 'Midsomer' countryside. Seven *Midsomer Murders* locations can be discovered on the River Chess Walk.

Chesham Museum, seen in 'Sins of Commission' and 17 Market Square, seen in 'Things that Go Bump in the Night'.

Chesham High Street, 'Causton' in 'The Axeman cometh'.

Chenies and Latimer

Until the thirteenth century, the present villages of Chenies and Latimer were one, albeit with the River Chess running through it. It was called Isenhampstead. However, in the reign of King Edward III the lands were split between two manorial barons, Thomas Cheyne and William Latimer.

Even in those days the barons had the equivalent of today's brand managers and the villages were called Isenhampstead Chenies and Isenhampstead Latimers. By the nineteenth century, the brand managers were getting smarter and Isenhampstead was dropped – no doubt because no one could spell it or even correctly pronounce it.

The villages are typical examples of a medieval feudal village that belonged to one landlord, the baron, who had total control over the village and its peasants. In the nineteenth century, at a time of great prosperity, most villages of this type were rebuilt.

Chenies, after its 'modernisation', was described as a 'beautiful specimen of an English village', a description that could still apply today.

From the beautiful village green with large shade trees, a gravel drive leads to the Manor House. Originally built in 1460 by the descendants of Thomas Cheyne, Chenies Manor House is now a Grade I listed building with, in my opinion, Grade I listed flower and herb gardens. Its fascinating history includes a ghost, reputed to be King Henry VIII!

The village church of St Michael is in a beautiful setting alongside the manor.

Nestling at the bottom of the Chess Valley, Latimer is a smaller village than Chenies, but as beautiful. Immaculate seventeenth- and eighteenth-century cottages surround its triangular village green. The green has a village pump, sadly no longer working, and a memorial to the soldiers who lost their lives in the Boer War.

Latimer's connection with the Boer War results from the fact that the third Baron Chesham, who resided at Latimer House, was a commander in the Boer War. His opposing Boer Commander, General Villebois De Mareuil, died in the war and the baron rescued his horse, also named Villebois, and brought it back to Latimer. It is still remembered today by a simple stone mound, inscribed 'Villebois', situated next to the Boer War memorial.

Left to right: Chenies Manor Gardens, seen in 'The Oblong Murders'; Villebois, the horse's memorial on Latimer Green; village pump, Latimer Green, a glimpse of which is seen in 'Death of a Hollow Man' and 'The Noble Art'; Black Hill Farm, seen in 'Strangler's Wood'.

FLAUDEN

'The village that moved'

SARRATT

'High and Dry'

The present-day Flauden is actually 'New' Flauden dating from the early nineteenth century. Old Flauden was close to the River Chess, actually too close, and after centuries of flooding the villagers decided to move to higher ground. Incidentally, it also moved from Buckinghamshire to Hertfordshire at the same time.

Flauden has the look of a modern Victorian village built around a crossroad. It lacks, as far as I can see, a green. In fact, the only green is the Green Dragon Inn.

Above: Flauden Cottage featured in 'Dance with the Dead'.

Left: The Green Dragon, also known as the 'The Airman' in 'Dance with the Dead'.

Right: River Chess.

The founders of Sarratt were smarter than their Flauden neighbours and settled on higher ground from the start. It is probably no coincidence that one of the meanings of the village's name is 'dry place'.

Sarratt appears to be all green. This, however, can be explained. In the seventeenth century, a development took place at the nearby hamlet, Sarratt Green, which expanded the hamlet in a straight line for nearly a mile to meet up with Sarratt. The developed linear village was called Sarratt Green. Eventually the 'Green' was dropped from the name but not in reality.

Sarratt is now the only location on the River Chess where watercress is grown. The remaining producer is a long way down a very narrow country lane, Moor Lane, which, believe it or not, is off the Sarratt road called The Green.

Buy some local watercress when you find the farm. It helps to keep this environmentally friendly industry alive. The watercress beds are open daily (and usually on Saturday mornings) for customers to buy this local-grown produce, which is rich in iron.

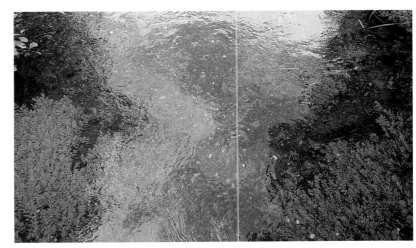

THE RIVER MISBOURNE AND METROLAND

AMERSHAM

'Seventeenth- and eighteenth-century magnificence'

The Amersham that features in *Midsomer Murders* is 'Old' Amersham, a historic market town situated in the valley of the River Misbourne, not the new town, Amersham-on-the-Hill.

Amersham has changed little since the seventeenth and eighteenth centuries. Stand by the Market Hall and admire the wide, slightly curving High Street and the coaching inns, which bear evidence to this. The reasons for this and the existence of Amersham-on-the-Hill owe much to Victorian Railwaymania and local resistance to the railways coming to their town.

In the late nineteenth century the Metropolitan Railway Company had grandiose plans to reach Paris by rail, as well as lesser plans to reach Amersham. They planned to reach Amersham along the Misbourne Valley but local resistance from landowners forced it to opt for Amersham Common, up the hill from Amersham, as the site for Amersham station.

The station opened in 1892 and the Metropolitan Railway, which owned large amounts of land along its route from London to Amersham Common, promoted the area along the line as 'Metro-Land'. It started to build houses and launched a very successful marketing campaign to attract people to live in 'London's nearest countryside'. The new town of Amersham-on-the-Hill was born and Amersham retained its character and affectionately became 'Old' Amersham.

Amersham was granted the rights to a market and fair in 1200. The market is held every Tuesday, but nowadays it is held in Amersham-on-the-Hill. The fun fair is still held every September in 'Old' Amersham.

Opposite page: Amersham High Street, seen in 'Death of a Hollow Man', 'Death in Disguise', 'Blue Herring', 'Who Killed Cock Robin?' and 'Sauce for the Goose'.

Britain in Bloom
Thames & Chilterns Region
Silver Gilt Award
Amersham 2010

Britain in Bloom
Thames & Chilterns Region
Gold Award
Amersham 2009

Britain in Bloom
Thames & Chilterns Region
Regional Town Winner
Amersham 2009

Britain in Bloom
Thames & Chilterns Region
Silver Gilt Award
Amersham 2008

Britain in Bloom
Thames & Chilterns Region
Silver Award
Amersham 2007

Amersham Market Hall, seen in many Midsomer Murders episodes.

Amersham Church.

The town's main trades were chair making and lace making. However, it was its location at the crossroads of trade routes that contributed greatly to its growth. Amersham was the first stop out of London for horse-drawn stagecoach travellers, resulting in it becoming a very important town with many coaching inns providing overnight accommodation and facilities to change the horses.

The Crown Inn and the Kings Arms are fine examples of coaching inns. Visit them, have a drink, a meal, close your eyes, let your imagination take hold of you and you will hear the clatter of horses' hoofs and the rattle of stagecoach wheels on cobblestones.

You could also imagine you had been here before. Amersham has been the location for many film and TV production scenes, including, of course, *Midsomer Murders*. Tours of the locations are available in the town.

The Amersham railway protesters of the nineteenth century and the twenty-first-century high-speed train objectors follow a long line of dissident Amersham inhabitants. During the Civil War, Oliver Cromwell's family lived in the area and from the seventeenth century prominent Quakers settled in the area and endured persecution. However, it was in support for the Reformation that seven Amersham inhabitants gave the ultimate sacrifice, their lives. On the hill above Old Amersham is The Martyrs' Memorial erected in memory to those who were burnt at the stake for their religious beliefs during the reign of Queen Mary. It is inscribed: 'In the shallow of depression at a spot 100 yards left of this monument seven Protestants, six men and one woman, were burned to death at the stake. They died for the principles of religious liberty, for the right to read and interpret the Holy Scriptures and to worship God according to their consciences as revealed through God's Holy Word'.

A glimpse of the Crown Hotel through Amersham Market Hall.

The Eagle Inn in bloom, Amersham.

LITTLE MISSENDEN

'The valley where marsh plants grow'

Lovely Little Missenden village, in beautiful Chiltern countryside, nestling around its ancient church of St John the Baptist and the River Misbourne chalk stream, has lost nothing of its charm and beauty over the centuries.

One feature of the church I have to mention: as you enter it, you are immediately aware of a remarkable thirteenth-century wall painting depicting St Christopher carrying Christ on his left shoulder.

It has a castle, well actually a little, low earthwork motte surrounded by the remains of a defensive ditch. The site in Chalk Lane, the other side of the by-pass, is just visible from the lane. Parking is difficult, so unless you are an enthusiast of little, low earthwork mottes, drive on by.

To add to its charm, Little Missenden has become a place for music and art. For well over fifty years the village has organised in October the Little Missenden Festival of Music and the Arts, which has built up a tradition of high-quality music-making in a unique Buckinghamshire village setting.

In the annals of *Midsomer Murders* Little Missenden ranks high. It was seen in the first episode 'The Killings at Badger's Drift' and it is believed that one of the suggested names for the series was 'Missenden Murders'.

GREAT MISSENDEN

'BFG and a by-passed church'

Great Missenden is best known as the home of the late Roald Dahl, the creator of the Big Friendly Giant (*The BFG*), *Matilda* and many other stories for children. The Roald Dahl Museum and Story Centre is situated in the High Street, a long curving street of half-timbered and Georgian shops, and a number of traditional pubs.

The village is overlooked by the medieval parish church of St Peter and St Paul. Its position away from the village raises the obvious question, why? I doubt that it has anything to do with the modern by-pass, which completely cuts off the church from the village. More like an earlier settlement around the church packing its bags and moving, for reasons and time unknown, to the present location.

Below: Left to right: St John the Baptist Church, Little Missenden; both the outside and inside were used in 'Echoes of the Dead'; Little Missenden cottages seen in 'The Killings at Badgers Drift', the very first Midsomer Murders episode and many subsequent episodes; Blacksmith, Great Missenden.

CHILTERN HUNDREDS AND THOUSANDS

CHILTERN HUNDREDS

'Outstanding beauty and a political sinecure'

Once upon a time English counties were divided into hundreds, a hundred being a measure of land having its own court and more importantly being a taxable area. In Buckinghamshire, the hilly wooded Chiltern Hills were divided into three hundreds, Stoke, Desborough and Burham. Nowadays the Chiltern Hundreds is used as a device to allow a member of the United Kingdom Parliament to resign.

Above: The Chilterns around Fingst, seen in 'Country Matters' and 'The Silent Land'.

Opposite page: Bluebells in Chiltern woodlands.

ALDBURY

'Woodlands, chalk downland and a canal'

Driving along the sun-dappled, wooded lanes of Ashridge Estate and down Toms Hill Lane, the view of a charming old English village, Aldbury, comes into sight.

The old stocks are next to the pond on the village green, which is surrounded by flower-bedecked cottages. The church is in the background, a whipping post is not far away and in the far corner is the Greyhound Inn, covered in a mass of summer flowers draping down from hanging baskets, pots and climbing plants.

Aldbury is almost completely surrounded by Ashridge Estate. The woodlands and chalk downland of the estate cover some 5,000 acres, with many thousands of trees. Open to the public throughout the year, the estate is perfect for short, long, easy and energetic walks, cycle rides on nearly 16,000 yards (9 miles) of public bridleways and horse riding, with permission, on over 26,000 yards (15 miles) of paths.

On the estate and overlooking Aldbury is a monument, erected in 1832, in honour of the third Duke of Bridgewater, acknowledged as the pioneer of British navigable canals. He commissioned the first British canal, the Bridgewater Canal near Manchester, and was one of the great visionaries of the eighteenth and nineteenth centuries.

I have a suspicion that the site of the monument was not chosen for its view, more likely that it was hidden from the view of Ashridge House. He was not the most liked member of the family. However, the view from the top of the monument would, I am sure, please the duke, as there is a good chance of seeing the Grand Union Canal near Tring.

Top right: Aldbury Church and the Ashridge Estate woodlands.

Bottom right: Aldbury Green and stocks seen in 'Written in Blood'.

THE LEE

The Lee, sitting on the Chiltern Hills above Great Missenden, is another one of those delightful clearings in the Chiltern Woods that suddenly opens up on your travels, exposing a beautiful village with its mandatory green. In fact, 'lee' is believed to be the old Anglo-Saxon word *leah* meaning 'woodland clearing'. Three other hamlets in the parish are simply named, Lee Clump, Lee Common and Lee Gate. What happened to Lee Bottom? The hamlet is known as Swan Bottom!

The manor is owned by the Liberty family, better known for their departmental store in Regent Street, London. You cannot miss the manor as the figurehead of HMS *Impregnable* guards the entrance.

A favourite with *Midsomer Murders*, The Lee has had several starring roles in the series. It was 'Badgers Drift' in 'The Killings at Badgers Drift' and 'Midsomer Florey' in 'Painted in Blood', which, believe it or not, only had one murder! In 2007 the village became 'Midsomer Holm', in 'Death in a Chocolate Box'.

Above right: The Cock and Rabbit, The Lee, also known as 'Safe Haven'.

Top right: The Lee, the original 'Badgers Drift'.

Bottom right: The camera obscura seen on The Lee village green in 'Death in a Chocolate Box' is sadly fictional.

PRESERVATION RAILWAY LINES

CHINNOR AND PRINCES RISBOROUGH RAILWAY

'Wrong kind of glue'

Chinnor is the home and only station of the Chinnor & Princes Risborough Railway, a preservation railway company operating a standard-gauge, steam and diesel-hauled train service on part of the old Great Western Railway branch line, which ran between Princes Risborough and Watlington. It is normally open to the public at weekends from March to October and in December for Santa Specials

The 3½-mile line runs along the foot of the Chiltern Hills, parallel to the Ridgeway, through beautiful countryside with outstanding views. As with all preservation railways, it offers cream teas, refreshments, a gift shop and 'Thomas the Tank Engine'.

A postbox was added to the station platform in the *Midsomer Murders*' episode 'Death in a Chocolate Box'. If you look carefully the postbox slightly rocks when a letter is placed inside it. 'Wrong kind of glue!'

At Wain Hill Halt the modern level crossing gates were only a temporary prop for this episode and the original ones have now been restored to their rightful position.

Opposite page: Bledlow Cricket Club in action as the diesel railcar seen in 'Death in a Chocolate Box' goes by.

Top right: Chinnor Station, also known as Holt Lane Junction in 'Death in a Chocolate Box', but no postbox.

Bottom right: Wain Hill crossing, the scene of a suicide in 'Death in a Chocolate Box'.

BUCKINGHAMSHIRE RAILWAY CENTRE

'Railwaymania to Railway Memorabilia'

Buckinghamshire Railway Centre is a working railway museum at Quainton Road railway station, which is as far as 'Metro-land' reached.

Amongst the static exhibits is Oxford Rewley Road station complete with Great Western Castle Class Express Passenger locomotive No. 5080, initially named *Ogmore Castle* but renamed in 1941 *Defiant*. Also exhibited is a dining car from the Royal Train of 1901, as well as another, reputedly used by General Eisenhower and Winston Churchill for wartime planning meetings.

The active exhibits range from passenger locomotives to shunting engines. There is also a miscellany of railway memorabilia providing a picture of how the advent of the railways changed the country's way of life.

Above: Old semaphore signals at Buckinghamshire Railway Centre, Quainton.

Opposite page: View from the railway bridge at Quainton as seen in 'Things that Go Bump in the Night' and 'Down Among the Dead Men'.

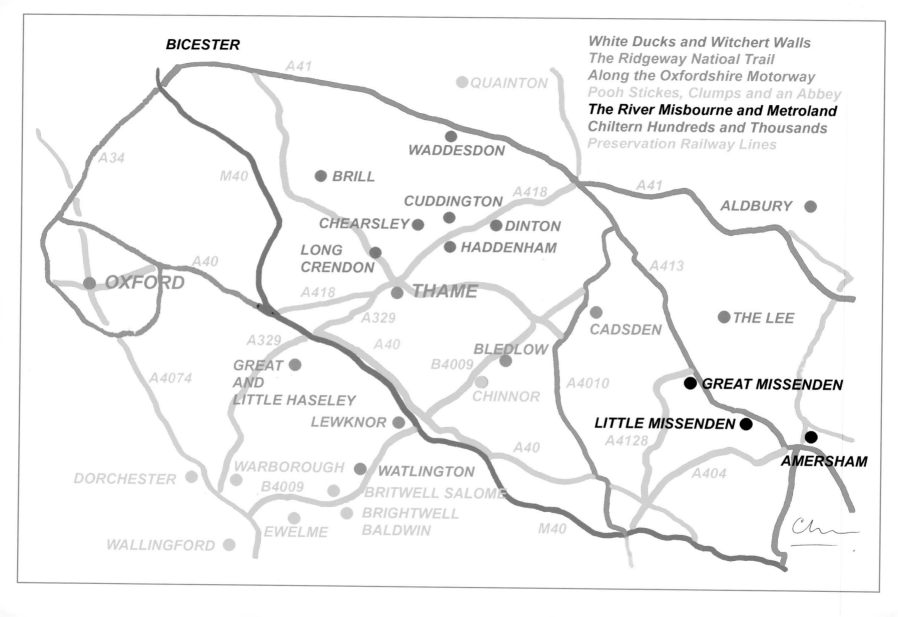

BICESTER

A41

QUAINTON

White Ducks and Witchert Walls
The Ridgeway Natioal Trail
Along the Oxfordshire Motorway
Pooh Stickes, Clumps and an Abbey
The River Misbourne and Metroland
Chiltern Hundreds and Thousands
Preservation Railway Lines

A34

WADDESDON

M40

BRILL

A418

CUDDINGTON

ALDBURY

CHEARSLEY

DINTON

A41

LONG
CRENDON

HADDENHAM

A413

A40

OXFORD

A418

THAME

A329

THE LEE

A329

A40

CADSDEN

GREAT
AND
LITTLE HASELEY

BLEDLOW

A4074

B4009

CHINNOR

A4010

GREAT MISSENDEN

LEWKNOR

LITTLE MISSENDEN

A4128

AMERSHAM

WARBOROUGH

WATLINGTON

A40

A404

DORCHESTER

B4009

BRITWELL SALOME

BRIGHTWELL
BALDWIN

EWELME

M40

WALLINGFORD

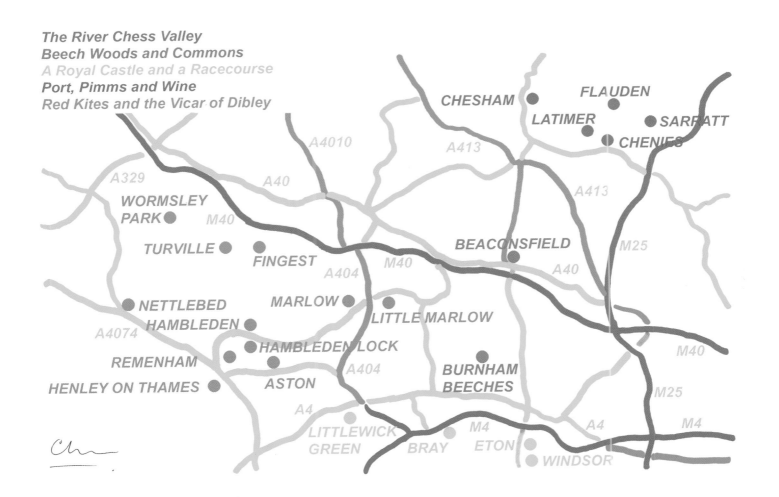

The River Chess Valley
Beech Woods and Commons
A Royal Castle and a Racecourse
Port, Pimms and Wine
Red Kites and the Vicar of Dibley

CHESHAM   FLAUDEN
    LATIMER   SARRATT
        CHENIES

A4010   A413

A329   A413

WORMSLEY
PARK   M40   M25
A40

TURVILLE   BEACONSFIELD
    FINGEST   A404   M40   A40

NETTLEBED   MARLOW   LITTLE MARLOW
HAMBLEDEN
A4074   HAMBLEDEN LOCK   M40

REMENHAM   A404   BURNHAM
                BEECHES
HENLEY ON THAMES   ASTON   M25
    A4
                        M4
    LITTLEWICK   M4   A4
    GREEN   BRAY   ETON
            WINDSOR

View across the valley of the River Thame towards Brill and Long Crendon.